The
TESTAMENT

By: **Lynn Matheson**

The Testament by Lynn Matheson © 2024

All rights reserved. No part of this book may be used or reproduced in any manner whatsoever, including internet usage, without written permission from Lynn Matheson except in the case of brief quotations embodied in critical articles and reviews.

Independently published in London, England.

TABLE OF CONTENTS

Preface 1

Chapter One: God 2

Chapter Two: The Universe 5

Chapter Three: Creation 7

Chapter Four: Life 9

Chapter Five: Spirits 11

Chapter Six: Incarnation of Spirits 13

Chapter Seven: The Soul After Death 15

Chapter Eight: Reincarnation 17

Chapter Nine: Mental Illness 23

Chapter Ten: Childhood 25

Chapter Eleven: Likes and Dislikes 27

Chapter Twelve: Forgetfulness 29

Chapter Thirteen: Freedom of the soul 31

Chapter Fourteen: Intervention of spirits in the material world 34

Chapter Fifteen: Missions of Spirits 36

Chapter Sixteen: The Three Divisions 37

Chapter Seventeen: Divine Law 39

Chapter Eighteen: Moral Perfection 52

Chapter Nineteen: Joys and Sorrows 55

Chapter Twenty: The Gospel According to Malalia 59

Chapter Twenty-ONE: Conclusion 65

Preface

This book contains information from my spirit guide who is called Malalia. She is a Venusian spiritual being. This text is a promise to humanity from God. It is a new form of Christianity. It is the original meaning of Jesus or Yeshua who came to Earth to teach a new way of living. His words were twisted so that his original meaning was lost.

Return to the Light.

CHAPTER ONE

GOD

God is the supreme intelligence. He is the first cause of all things. He was there at the beginning. He did not come into being. He just is. He always was and always will be. He is neither male nor female. Using He as God's pronoun is just a convention. We will use "He" in this book, but He is both the masculine and the feminine energy. God is infinite in His perfection. It is impossible to explain God adequately to the human mind. If you saw Him, it would damage your brain. He can only be understood when you are in spirit form. After death you will come to more understanding of God. He is infinite: He has neither beginning nor end. He exists as a real and separate entity. He is not the same as the universe. He created the universe. He is both within and without. Some people call Him Source or other such names. The name does not matter. The word for God that Yeshua (Jesus) used is 'Abwoon'. This is an Aramaic word. Abwoon has the sense of oneness and of birthing and breath. It is a suitable name to use for God. Abwoon breathed the world into existence.

There is nothing without a cause. You see the law of cause and effect all around you in the world. You kick a ball, and it moves. The sun rises in the morning and gives light to the world. The baby cries and the mother comforts him. The guard dog barks, and the thieves withdraw. The tides move in and out according to the actions of the moon. The plants grow towards the light. The universe was caused by God. This is the proof. Every effect has a cause. Something cannot come from nothing.

All peoples from the beginning of time have had a feeling in their minds that God exists. You see the idea of God in all cultures and time periods. Many of the ancient cultures had a more sophisticated idea of God than we do today. You see God in The Aboriginal culture of Australia, in the Native American cultures, in the peoples of the desert and those of the tropics. You see God represented in the earliest of times: the Druids of England and France, the Vikings of Scandinavia, the Hindus of India, the Aztecs of South America, the peoples of Africa. Not all peoples had the right idea of God, but they sensed that there was something more than the material world. Many ancient cultures worshipped many gods. This was an error. There is only one God. The gods some people worshipped were often angels or other kinds of spiritual beings. Some were aliens who visited Earth. They were not gods but messengers of God. There are many high and holy spirits. People can call them angels. There are also mischievous beings who like to play tricks on people. These were often worshipped as gods, but they were not gods. Some people call these beings demons but that is incorrect. They are spiritual beings who are not yet advanced in nature. They tend to do evil things and lead people up the wrong path.

It is only in recent times that doubts have crept in due to the advancements of science in the existence of God. Modern scientific ideas regarding God are incorrect if they are wholly material in nature. The universe did not occur by chance. God willed it into being. The harmony behind the workings of the universe suggests an intelligent creator. Everything has a place and is working towards the greater good even though we cannot understand this as human beings in 3D reality. Everything has its place in the divine order. The humble house fly is performing a useful task as is the king on his throne.

The wonders of the world you perceive means the creator of such a place must be extremely intelligent, more intelligent than any person we could think of. We can all look at the beauty of a sunset or the light dancing on the waters of a lake. We feel the beauty of the world. Some scientists are blinded by their own arrogance. They do not understand as much as they pretend. This arrogance is a fault in people. Eventually, scientific ideas will be corrected, and people will know the truth. Even today this correction is already happening. There is a spiritual dimension to the universe along with the material. Physics is advancing all the time and scientists change their ideas according to new discoveries. The Big Bang theory which purports to explain how the universe came into being has several problems and things it cannot adequately explain. Explanations of the universe will come from string theory and quantum physics as they develop.

God is perfection but language cannot do justice to describe Him. He is eternal, infinite, unchangeable, immaterial, unique, omnipotent and good. There is only one God. He is not just the universe. God is the creator and the creation. His intelligence is revealed in His works. Think of Him like an artist creating a painting. The skill and beauty of the painting shows how great the artist is. Look around at the world and you will feel awe in its beauty and power.

There are many who Say God cannot be good because of the evil in the world. The universe only appears evil because you have limited perception. You cannot understand the whole if you are incarnated within a body.

God is in the things of the world and in human beings. Each human soul is a part of the divine. Souls are created by God. Each person has an immortal soul. God is also in the rocks, the sea and the earth. Ancient peoples often had the idea of God dwelling within all things: animism. There is some truth in animism, but God also resides externally to things as well as dwelling within them.

CHAPTER TWO
THE UNIVERSE

Humans can never understand how the universe works. They are not yet evolved enough to understand it. As people purify themselves, they will know more. People can purify themselves by becoming good: thinking good thoughts and doing good actions. Meditation helps people to come to a better understanding of their world. People can also use prayer.

Science helps people to understand how things work but so many scientists suffer from arrogance and pride. These qualities stop them from understanding the true nature of things and they spread many untruths. As understanding grows, so should admiration for the Creator. Sadly, this adulation does not always happen. In fact, the reverse is true, and many scientists are atheists and persuade other people to atheism. They are in the wrong.

The universe is made up of matter and spirit. Not all matter can be perceived with the human senses. Spirit contains intelligence but it is not only intelligence. The world is both material and immaterial. There is a universal substance which stands between spirit and matter. You might call it the electromagnetic field or the quantum field. You can think of it like a liquid.

The universe is infinite. We cannot conceive of it ending because then there would have to be something outside of it.

CHAPTER THREE
CREATION

The universe contains many worlds. We are not aware of all of them. There are many that have not yet been discovered. Some are immaterial and cannot be detected with human instruments. They are spiritual worlds. There are beings living on many planets in the material plane and in the spiritual plane. There are other races of beings on other planets and other star systems. You might call them aliens. You would be alien to them. They are different from you as their conditions of living are different. The beings on other worlds are different to human beings. Some are more advanced than humans and some are less advanced. They have different ways of eating and of reproducing. The universe was created by God. He willed it into being.

The worlds within the universe are constantly coming into being and ceasing to exist. At the beginning of the Earth there was chaos and then things settled into what we see today. Plants and animals appeared gradually according to their proper time from the substances contained within the Earth itself. Then human beings appeared in the same way.

The book of Genesis in the Bible is a simplified, allegorical version of events. It should not be taken as the literal truth. The Earth did not take six days to create but things appeared over long time periods. Adam was not the first man, but he did exist and founded the Jewish race. There were many races in existence before him. Human life sprang up in different times and places all over the globe.

The days of creation in Genesis were not literal days but referred to thousands of years of evolution. The flood described in Genesis did not destroy the whole Earth but was just a local event. Care should be taken when reading the Bible that you do not take its words as literal truth. This advice is good for all the spiritual writings in the religions of the world. They have some of the truth but not all of it. Spiritual texts are more like poetry than scientific tracts.

CHAPTER FOUR

LIFE

There are organic and inorganic beings. Organic beings have life like people, animals and plants. Some beings are inorganic and have no life in them. These are rocks, water and air. The vital principle of life has its origins in the universal fluid or the quantum field. This fluid links spirit and matter.

Organic beings die when their organs wear out. The universal fluid joins back from where it came from. You can think of it like a battery gradually being wound down. The soul goes back to the spiritual world. After a review of the most recent life the soul is reincarnated into a new body to learn new lessons.

Intelligence comes from the universal intelligence. Substances like minerals do not have intelligence. The plants also do not have intelligence, but they have vitality. Then there are beings that are intelligent and have vitality. Animals and people can think. Animals use instinct which is a form of intelligence. Humans have instinct too, but we tend to ignore it. If we listen to it, then it will serve us well. People can be led astray by over-use of reason. Reason gives people free will. They must guard against too much pride and selfishness when using their reasoning powers. It can lead them to do the wrong thing.

CHAPTER FIVE

SPIRITS

Spirits are the intelligent beings of creation. Spirits are created by God. We are God's children. How this happens is not for us to know. It cannot be explained to humans. Spirits are always being created. Spirits are everywhere. You are surrounded by spirits all the time but most of you cannot perceive them. The life of a spirit has no end.

Spirits vary in their level of purity. Some are more advanced, and they seek perfection. Others are lowly due to their love of evil and passions. Many of these spirits are not yet ready to learn the higher things. If you could see them their colours are different. Some might be grey while purer souls can be red. They also might appear like flames. They can travel enormous distances quickly. Spirits can decide to appear to you in a form you can perceive. This could be in dreams or visions.

There are spirits who enjoy doing bad things. There are also mischievous spirits who like to play tricks on humans. Not all spirits have knowledge of things just because they are spirits. Some know very little. Low spirits enjoy deceiving people and encouraging them to do bad actions. They can attach themselves to people. The low spirits can pretend to have more knowledge than they possess which can mislead people. They also enjoy rapping and moving objects. These are the kind of spirits you may encounter in a séance or using a Ouija board.

The high spirits have knowledge and moral excellence to varying degrees. They enjoy doing good. They may put good thoughts into human minds. These spirits are still undergoing a process of purification, so they have their own trials to undergo. Human beings may have these spirits dwelling within them. These people do good for its own sake. They are kind and do not show pride, selfishness nor ambition. They are not full of hate or envy. Some of these good spirits excel in kindness while others are more interested in knowledge. Some are wise. There are those who combine all these qualities. These high spirits will communicate with people who have open hearts and want genuine knowledge. The highest of these beings are known as angels, archangels or seraphim. They have achieved perfection and serve God. They are God's messengers and contribute to the harmony of the universe.

All spirits are in the process of perfecting themselves. Some are quicker than others. God does not create good and evil spirits. He creates spirits that are simple but ignorant. They choose evil themselves. Every spirit has free will. Some spirits will try to lead a person astray. People talk about this temptation as Satan, but it is really the low spirits. Every spirit will eventually attain perfection. Evil ways will be left behind.

God does not create evil spirits who we call demons. No spirits are damned for all eternity. The demons are just impure spirits but the state they find themselves in is only temporary. Satan or the Devil does not exist in the way people have thought. The Bible is an allegory and often uses metaphorical language that is not to be taken literally. There is no hell.

CHAPTER SIX
INCARNATION OF SPIRITS

Spirits incarnate so that they can attain perfection. For some it is a way of atoning for past wrongdoing. It can also be a mission. To attain perfection a spirit must go through every bodily experience. Incarnation is a way the spirit can contribute to the work of creation as well as increasing his own advancement. Spirits are on a journey towards God. If they do good actions, then they arrive at the destination more quickly. Spirits suffer more when they are imperfect. Overcoming envy, jealousy and avarice will ensure less suffering.

A soul is an incarnate spirit. Before the soul was in the body it was a spirit. Therefore, souls are spirits. They incarnate into a human body temporarily to achieve more purity and enlightenment. There is in each one of us a link between the soul and the body. This link is halfway between the material and the immaterial. You can call it the perispirit. It allows the soul to act on the body and the body to act on the soul. The soul leaves the body at death. A spirit cannot inhabit two bodies at once.

If you communicate with spirits some will give you incorrect information. Some spirits cannot understand advanced abstract ideas and others have learned the wrong information. Still others find it hard to express their meaning within the limits of human language. In this way, incorrect information can be given to mediums. Care must be taken that you are communication with a high spiritual being, not a low or mischievous one.

Scientists tend to become materialists and deny the spiritual world. This tendency is due to pride. They think they know everything and that nothing can be hidden from them. Disbelief in the spiritual plane has negative consequences. In such a world, every man thinks only of himself, and everything becomes about satisfying his material desires. Looking around the world today we see this is happening more and more. It is not making for happy people or a happy world. There is a need for morality for society to function well. At the current time there are many wars going on and people in the wealthier countries are becoming more and more materially minded. We must change by returning our thoughts to God.

Communication with spirits can allow us to see the afterlife. We can see that we are immortal beings that are not annihilated after death. We can be assured of future happiness.

CHAPTER SEVEN

THE SOUL AFTER DEATH

At the moment of death, the soul becomes a spirit. The soul keeps its sense of individuality. It has its own fluid which is like the appearance of its last incarnation. The soul remembers its last life, but it desires to go to a better world. Advanced souls are purer, and they understand the futility of much on Earth. Some say the soul returns to the universal whole and loses its individuality, but this reasoning is incorrect. Souls are not like drops of water in the ocean. They are individuals which are part of the whole. The spirits have natures as various as human beings do. Some are serious, some silly, some learned, some ignorant. Spirits live eternally. Only the body dies.

When the soul leaves the body there is no pain in the process. The spirit feels joy that it is returning home. It is just like a candle flame going out. The process is not always instantaneous. The separation can take some time. On entry to the spirit world a spirit that has done evil things will feel shame. A spirit that has followed a good path feels like he has dropped a heavy load. The spirit is greeted by those who he knew on

Earth. He may also meet his spirit guides. The spirit may feel confused for a time and not realise what has happened to it. Purified spirits understand the separation much more easily. Those who have not clung to material pursuits find the separation easier to understand.

CHAPTER EIGHT
REINCARNATION

Each soul is trying to purify itself. This life is an attempt to purify itself. If the process of purification is not complete, then the soul can undergo a new existence. We call this reincarnation. The goal of reincarnation is the improvement of people. It is also about atonement: making amends for wrongdoing. Each incarnation allows the soul to improve. Eventually, he has attained enough purity to need no further lives. Some spirits advance more quickly than others. After the last incarnation, the spirit is in a state of bliss.

God allows reincarnation as he is just. There is always the possibility of repentance. God does not sentence anyone to eternal suffering. This would be unfair. People are placed in circumstances over which they have no control. Some lives make it difficult for the soul to advance. There is always another chance in another life. Each soul can redeem itself through new trials.

Reincarnation offers hope to everyone. Don't lose heart because you have made mistakes. There is always another chance. Each experience he has learned from will help him in the next life.

Spirits can incarnate in a whole host of different worlds, not just on Earth. The current Earth is one of the most imperfect worlds so anyone incarnating here is having a tough trial. Souls may have many lives on Earth until they are ready to move on to a different world. If a spirit did not incarnate, he would not move forward in his purification and so would not move closer to God. Each time a soul comes back to Earth he is placed in a different set of circumstances so that he can learn new lessons. Spirits never go backwards in their process of purification, but they can remain at the same point. If they have been rebellious, they must learn lessons in a new existence. If a spirit fails in his mission, he will undergo the same kind of life again. Spirits have bodies in the other worlds just like in this one. If the spirit is more advanced than others his body will be less material. Purer spirits may live in less material worlds. More purified spirits live in worlds where there is no need to kill animals for food. They have fewer animal passions and so are much less selfish than most people on Earth. They have no need of war.

The pure spirits live in their own special worlds, but they can also move between any of the worlds instantaneously. There is life on all the other planets even though we are not aware of it. Earth is one of the least advanced of all the planets. Venus is more advanced than Earth and Mars is less advanced. The aliens who live on Venus and Mars are not material beings. They are in a spiritual state though they can materialise if they wish. They are in another dimension.

When a spirit is first created it is not advanced. It is like a baby. It learns more through each incarnation. First, the passions are developed. Each spirit must pass through each stage until it reaches perfection. These stages cannot be rushed or passed over. Even if you try to live perfectly in this lifetime you may not have achieved perfection as the spirit world sees it. Spirits can never go backwards in their development. They are always striving for perfection. Moral advancement has nothing to do with social position. A great soul can be born into the body of a farm labourer. Often, it is the case that the greatest spirits are found in humble circumstances. Jesus was a carpenter. Nero was an Emperor. Who was the better soul?

To improve your spirit, you need to avoid evil and do good. The spirit is all that matters, and the body is of no account. It is just like a piece of clothing which you can remove.

Babies who die young may be wiser than their parents. They may have lived many more previous lives. The child could be in a state of high advancement because of the progress he made in his previous lives. The early death of the child could be to do with a lesson that the parents need to learn. Everyone has a chance to advance because God is a just and loving God. The child will be reincarnated. Children are capable of passions and wrongdoing. This is because their spirits are not advanced. They are here to learn lessons so that their soul can evolve.

A spirit can incarnate as a man or woman. They all do both. Incarnating as both men and women gives them a greater variety of experience so they can learn more lessons. Spirits themselves do not have a sex. A child's parents only give him the body. The spirit that inhabits the child is not to do with them. We may meet people in this life whom we have had relationships with before. This is why you may feel dislike of someone on first meeting or even feel that you love them at first sight.

Your job in this life is to do good. Follow the example of good in your family but don't follow those who do evil. Spirits will often choose to incarnate among people they feel in harmony with though this is not always the case. Some spirits may choose to be born into a difficult family as a test or a trial. They will give lessons to the family. An advanced spirit is not always in a beautiful body. A spirit may choose a deformed physical appearance.

A spirit may have some inkling of things he has learned in his previous lives. It can seem like he has some innate ideas. He might feel this in the form of intuition. When he leaves the body, the spirit will remember everything he has learned.

The idea of reincarnation has been held by many peoples from the very earliest times. You see it in Hinduism which is an ancient religion. The idea of continual lives means everyone has many chances to improve himself. Christianity does not currently accept the doctrine of reincarnation, but the early Church did believe in such a thing. With an accumulation of evidence perhaps the Church will accept the reality of reincarnation. The notion does not damage Christianity but rather enhances it. Jesus himself spoke about reincarnation. When he came down from the mountain after the transfiguration, he warned his disciples not to speak of it until he has resurrected. They disciples ask him why the scriptures say that Elijah must come first. Jesus says that Elijah has already returned but nobody recognised him. Elijah was reincarnated as John the Baptist.

A soul can be reincarnated almost immediately after separation from the body but usually there is an interval of time between incarnations. A spirit without a body is a wandering spirit who is waiting to be reborn. It could be a matter of earth hours or thousands of years. A spirit could be studying during this time to help his advancement. There are pure spirits who do not need to incarnate again. Pure spirits do visit the lower worlds to help them to move forward. They act as spirit guides.

As spirits advance their knowledge increases. Less advanced spirits may know very little. The sense of time means very little to spirits so there is no point asking them about dates and time predictions. Decades of time to us seem just like an instant to them. Advanced spirits may be able to see the future to some degree. They may not be allowed to reveal the future they perceive to human beings. Spirits can move as fast as our thoughts move so they can see the whole Earth at once. Spirits can see very clearly, and they also perceive sounds. They have no need of rest, and they cannot feel physical suffering as they have no body. Spirits can suffer from mental distress. Those who have lived a good life will suffer much less than those who have given into excess desires and carnality.

Some sufferings a human being endures on Earth are because of the plan they made before they were born. However, they do not choose all the details which will happen due to the choices they make on Earth. A spirit may choose to be born among bad people as a trial so he can learn to overcome something. You could choose a life of poverty to bear it with fortitude or in contrast you could choose riches to try to overcome the evil doings which may arise from having such a fortunate situation.

Giving into the animal instincts always leads to bad consequences. The choice of a painful life that is borne with a good heart will allow the spirit to advance more rapidly. People who have been proud on Earth may find in the spirit world they are of the lowest rank. Those who have led humble lives will be the highest ranking of spirits.

Spirits communicate with each other by a kind of telepathy. They recognise each other and have individuality. Good people will be welcomed into the spirit world by those who love them. Spirits tend to stay with those who are at the same level of advancement.

The idea of a twin flame or a soul mate that you are fated to meet to feel complete is not true. All spirits are united. No soul is incomplete on its own. You feel sympathetic to other spirits according to their degree of advancement. Spirits on the same level as each other will tend to gravitate together.

Spirits can remember all their past lives and often laugh at their wrong doings and faulty understanding. They shed their bodies like a cumbersome garment. A spirit does not care about the decomposition of his body as it is no longer important to him. Higher spirits do not miss the material pleasures of human life. They enjoy the happiness of the spirit world. They don't worry about what they have left behind as they know others will continue their work. Often what seemed important to them on Earth is not important when they are in spirit. They don't feel a particular affinity with their home country as they are happiest among spirits at the same level as them. Spirits like to be remembered with affection, but they do not give much importance to graves or monuments. They like to be remembered with the heart; the place is unimportant. Spirits sometimes attend their own funerals.

All spirits eventually choose to reincarnate due to the need to advance themselves. Some put off the experience for a long time while others return immediately. A spirit may choose his body or have it chosen for him. He may choose a deformed body to learn a lesson. Each life will have trials that he must undergo to advance. The spirit can feel anxious about achieving his goals in the new incarnation. The spirit may have friends who accompany him into his new life. You might see spirit friends in dreams.

The soul unites with the body at conception or soon after. Often it is between the third and the sixth month. The link between the body and the soul becomes stronger and stronger as birth approaches. Sometimes the link can be broken if the spirit withdraws. In this case the child would not live. If a spirit chooses a body that dies prematurely then he just chooses another body. Often this premature death happens because of something being wrong with the matter of the body. An infant who only lives for a few days is providing a lesson for the parents. Sometimes the spirit may find the burden of the life he has chosen too heavy and may commit suicide. As birth approaches the spirit forgets his life in the spirit world.

Every child that survives its birth has a spirit incarnated within it. If an abortion takes place, then the incarnation must be attempted again in another body. Abortion is a crime. It goes against the laws of God. A soul has been prevented by the abortion from undergoing its trials. If there is a possibility of danger to the baby or the mother a decision must be made that takes account of the highest good of all.

The purer the spirit that is inhabiting inside the body then the more likely the person will be inclined to moral acts. Nobody is wholly bad but rather in a state of imperfection. It is possible for a human to be extremely intelligent but also have evil inclinations. This happens when the spirit still has a lot of purification to do. Nobody has several spirits within him but just one. Each spirit has a unique personality and identity.

Matter is only the envelope of the spirit like wearing clothes. The spirit in the body still retains its spiritual nature. The spirit can be weakened by the grossness of the body. The spirit feels like it is in dirty water. It cannot exercise its faculties freely. The development of the bodily organs is an effect not a cause of the spirit.

CHAPTER NINE
MENTAL ILLNESS

Every being has a soul. Those who are considered lacking in intelligence or mentally ill will often have an intelligent soul. It just finds it cannot communicate effectively because of a deficiency of the body. A spirit that finds himself in such a body is undergoing a punishment. They are suffering as they cannot achieve what they wish with the organs they have been given. It is as if he is an excellent musician who has been given a faulty instrument so he cannot play as well as he would like.

A spirit with a healthy body and brain can overcome the obstacles that are placed in his way. If the matter is resistant as in the case of a lack of intelligence or mental illness, then the spirit cannot achieve what he intends. A body may be so damaged that it cannot do anything much, neither good nor evil. The soul is having a break in its advancement. It could be that it is to make up for wrongdoing in another incarnation. A person of low intelligence may have been a genius in a previous incarnation.

If there is a fault within the brain the spirit cannot achieve its intentions. It's just the same as someone who is blind because of a fault with the eyes or someone who cannot walk because of an imperfection in the legs. Sometimes a spirit will choose suicide because he cannot manifest what he wants with the faulty brain. After death, the spirit may feel confused for a while. It is as if he can still feel the burden of mental illness. Healing can take place before the next incarnation.

CHAPTER TEN
CHILDHOOD

A great advanced spirit may inhabit the body of a child. The child's brain is not fully developed so he cannot think like an adult. A child is confused until its organs develop fully when it can then achieve what the spirit desires. If a child dies the spirit goes back to the spirit world. It might take some time for the spirit to fully recover. The connection between the spirit and the body lessens over time.

The spirit is in a state of rest during childhood waiting for the organs to develop fully. A spirit can receive impressions during childhood which will help the soul to advance. A baby cries at birth to attract the attention of his mother so that he can receive the care he needs.

The spirit can show itself more once the child is becoming an adult. Children are given the appearance of innocence so that adults care for them. Parents who believe their children to be innocent, good and gentle will give them all the love and care they need. The real character of a child will appear as he approaches maturity. The weakness of the stage of childhood allows the child to be amenable to the advice of caring adults. Evil inclinations can be suppressed, and the child is guided to good acts. It is of the utmost importance to educate a child morally. Childhood is a natural part of the laws of God.

CHAPTER ELEVEN
LIKES AND DISLIKES

There may be spirits who have known each other in previous lives. They would not recognise each other in this life but they may well be attracted to each other. The two spirits may unconsciously seek each other among people so it seems as if fortune has brought them together. It is not always true that love comes from previous lives. Spirits that are in harmony will seek each other naturally.

Sometimes two spirits may instinctively dislike one another. The spirits have recognised each other's nature without the need for words. The fact that two spirits dislike each other does not mean that one is evil. It can just be that the two spirits are not in harmony. As they become more advanced souls the dislike disappears.

A bad spirit may feel dislike for someone who may judge and unmask him. Hatred and jealousy can come from being aware of the other person's disapproval. A good spirit may also feel repulsion for a bad one. He knows that the two will have nothing in common. In a good spirit hatred or jealousy will not manifest but the good spirit will avoid or pity the bad one.

CHAPTER TWELVE
FORGETFULNESS

When a spirit incarnates, he loses all memory of the spirit world. This forgetfulness happens because God does not want people to know everything. If a human being could see the true reality, he would be completely dazzled by it. There must be a veil which keeps certain things hidden. Through forgetting the past, the person can concentrate fully on this life.

Sometimes people will argue that it would make more sense for progression and advancement if one could remember wrongdoing of past lives so he can profit from the experience of this one. It seems like we are starting from scratch each time. The answer is that with each new incarnation the spirit becomes more intelligent. He is also more able to distinguish between good and evil. He has true freedom because he cannot remember his past lives.

When the spirit returns to the spirit world, he sees all his past actions. He understands what he could have done to avoid them. He seeks out a new life to repair the mistakes of the old one. He asks for spirit guides to aid him in the task. The spirit guide gives feeling and intuitions to help the person choose good actions. Evil thoughts arise and can be resisted by exercising the conscience. This conscience is the voice of the past encouraging the person not to fall into the same faults of the past.

The goal is to undergo trials with fortitude and to resist temptation. By doing this the spirit advances to a higher level.

There are other worlds where the beings there can remember all their past lives. They are happy as they understand God's creation. There are people who live in favourable conditions on Earth who are still unhappy because they do not remember the discomforts of previous lives. In advanced worlds the past lives are only considered like an unpleasant dream. In this world, these memories would affect us too much. God has ordered the universe in the best way so that we do not suffer too much by remembering past suffering.

There are people on Earth who can remember their past lives. The past life may appear in a dream, but one needs to be careful as in some cases it is just the imagination. Deep hypnosis can also help a person to see their past lives. An experience meditator can also see their past lives. In worlds where the body is less material past lives can be remembered more easily.

Each spirit is trying to advance himself by overcoming his trials. If he succeeds, he goes up a grade. If he fails, he must try again. A spirit always has free will to choose between good and evil. If he did not have free will he would be no better than a machine.

Sometimes, the higher spirits will allow someone to see their past lives. This is because it will help to achieve a higher purpose. It should only be done for a reason not just for entertainment.

Each incarnation will try to atone for the shortcomings of the past lives. A proud person will be given a lowly position in the next life. A person who lusted after wealth will live in poverty. A person who has been idle will have to undergo constant labour.

CHAPTER THIRTEEN
FREEDOM OF THE SOUL

The spirit inside the body desires to be free. It is always active. During sleep the spirit can travel to other locations and communicate with other spirits. Dreams give us an inkling of the life of the spirit while we are asleep. Memory of the past and prophecy of the future is possible. A strange dream which you do not understand may be a memory of a past life. It could even be a life in the future or on another planet. The soul is partially freed from the body during sleep. It is the same as what happens after death when the soul is completely free of the body. Death is nothing to fear as you die every day when you go to sleep.

Through sleep, incarnated spirits are connected to the spirit world. Dreams can give you some idea about the spirit world, but you don't always remember what you have seen. Dreams can also be confused by the entry or the exit from the spiritual world. Caution must be exercised about dreams as bad spirits can use them against you.

Some people can remember the spirit world completely. They are often people who are at an advanced spiritual level such as Hindu mystics or prophets from the Bible. Jesus was one such person. Buddha also came to know the truth of the spiritual world.

Often, we cannot remember our dreams because the matter of the body is so heavy, so it is difficult to remember the impressions given during sleep as these impressions were not received through the organs of the body.

Dreams may not foretell the future though in some cases they do. They may be remembering the past or prophesying the future. It may also be possible to see something happening in another place. People may appear to their relatives and friends in dreams. Spirits can come to visit you and you can go to visit them. A spirit may communicate you with words that stay with you upon waking. Though you may forget these dreams the spirit remembers them, and you may receive the knowledge in the form of inspiration during the day. The incarnated spirit may have a presentiment about his own death. A spirit may also cause the body to feel fatigued.

People who know each other can visit each other during sleep. People who do not know each other in the material world can also visit each other during slumber. When people have the same idea at the same time this is often because spirits are communicating with each other.

When people are in a coma the spirit is still active and attached to the body. It can only leave the body when the body is completely dead. If someone appears to be dead but comes to life again it is because they were not dead.

Some people have clairvoyant abilities, and they can see like a spirit sees. They are not seeing through the organs of the body. Clairvoyants are not permitted to see everything, and they can be influenced by their own prejudices. What they say must be treated with care.

Spiritually advanced people may have ecstatic visions where they experience the higher states. Care must still be taken as it is possible that a person is being deceived by lower spirits.

Some people have the gift of seeing the future or receive information from the spiritual world. This can occur spontaneously, but people can also train themselves to thin the veil between the worlds. Second sight can run in families because the people within the family are having similar experiences and training each other without realising it. Some people develop special abilities when they have undergone a great trauma such as a near death experience or a stressful time of powerful emotions.

When a psychic is in touch with the spiritual world he is speaking as a soul. His spirit may leave his body to see other places and times or communicate with other spirits. This kind of activity seems to prove the existence of the soul as the psychic can say things which he could not possibly know and even things beyond his intellectual capacity. In trance, the soul is independent of the body.

CHAPTER FOURTEEN

INTERVENTION OF SPIRITS IN THE MATERIAL WORLD

Spirits are always around you. They can see everything you see though they may choose not to. You cannot hide anything from the spirits. Frivolous spirits may delight in causing you annoyances. More serious spirits will pity your flaws and try to help you overcome them. Spirits do influence our thoughts and actions. Some ideas that come into your mind may come from the spirits. You must use discernment with ideas from the spirits. Imperfect spirits want you to suffer because they suffer. They may give you bad advice. Anything that takes you further away from God is a bad idea.

God allows the spirits to incite us to evil as a test of our faith. You pass through trials so that you can obtain ultimate goodness. You can free yourself from the influence of malign spirits by changing your thoughts.

Think virtuous thoughts and do good actions. The spirits with evil intent will then leave you alone. Put all your faith in God.

People cannot be possessed by a spirit in the sense that there can never be two spirits in the same body. However, a soul can be dominated by another spirit so that its will is paralysed. It is always possible to shake off the influence of evil spirits. Prayer can help but the person must make a sincere effort to cure himself of his defects.

Good spirits also take an interest in us and may do all they can to help us. They seek to inspire us to turn our trials into good fortune. Relatives and friends who have died before us may take an interest in us and can try to protect us.

Everyone has a guardian angel which is another way of saying a protective spirit. Some people call these beings spirit guides. This kind of spirit is like a parent. He tries to give advice and to console us in our sorrows and to give us courage to undergo our trials. The guardian angel is with you from birth to death. You should talk to your guardian angel often. Question them and develop an affectionate friendship. You cannot lie to them. They see everything. The goal of guardian angels is to bring you closer to God.

By communicating constantly with your guardian angel, you become a medium and the aim is for everyone on earth to be a medium. When you have received the right instruction, you can then raise others around you. Helping others on the road to eternal bliss is the task you have been given by God.

People who ask for aid from evil spirits are doing the wrong thing. They may gain earthly pleasures, but they will pay for it later in the spirit world. They will have more work to do to make their actions right.

You cannot make an evil spell against another person. God does not allow this. Belief in such things is just superstition. People may fall ill from a spell purely because they believe in it rather than any inherent magic in the spell itself.

CHAPTER FIFTEEN
MISSIONS OF SPIRITS

Spirits take part in the harmony of the universe. They carry out the wishes of God. They are constantly occupied but they never get tired, and they don't need to consider the needs of their bodies as they don't have them. Every spirit has a duty to fulfil. Even the highest spirits do not have eternal repose but carry out orders directly from God. Each spirit is trying to attain the highest perfection.

We cannot understand all the missions. Each spirit must make himself useful. If a person is wilfully idle, he will suffer for it in this life or in others. The best thing is to try to advance your fellow beings.

CHAPTER SIXTEEN

THE THREE DIVISIONS

The natural world is divided into mineral, vegetable and animal by many people. Some say there are two classes: organic and inorganic. As regards morality there are four types: inert matter, plants, animals, humans. Plants are not conscious of their existence. They receive physical impressions, but they do not feel pain. Plants do not think and have no will. They only have instinct causing them to move in certain directions.

Man is not an animal. He is a being apart. He sometimes sinks very low and sometimes raises himself very high. Man is superior to animals because he has the idea of the existence of God.

Animals act from instinct but they also have will. They use their intelligence to satisfy their physical needs and to preserve their own existence. Animals do have a kind of soul, but it is not the same as a human soul.

Humans are the only beings who can truly know God.

The doctrine of metempsychosis regarding animals is not true. This term is the idea that spirits will reincarnate into a different species. A spirit that has incarnated in a human body can never go back to being an animal. The animals have their own path and we have ours. You cannot be reincarnated as a beetle or a dog. You can only be reincarnated as another human. Some religions have taught the idea that you can be reborn as an animal, but they are mistaken.

CHAPTER SEVENTEEN
DIVINE LAW

The law of nature is the same as the law of God. Man can be happy when he follows the law of God. God has established laws that last for all of eternity. They cannot be changed.

To understand God's law, you should seek after goodness. Enlightenment is obtained through the experience of many lifetimes.

The law of God resides in each person's conscience. Some people have the mission of revealing God's law to others. Most men have forgotten the law or do not understand it. A true prophet is an upright person who is inspired by God. His goodness is apparent in his words and his deeds.

Jesus is an example of a moral, upright person. His teachings are the purest expression of the divine law. He was a pure being. Some of his teachings in the Bible are not actually things that he said. The Bible has been changed by many different people for their own purposes. The emperor Constantine held a council where he decided what was to be included in the Bible and what was not. He came to agreement with the bishops and priests and other important people of the time. Some of the content was changed to fit in with more typical Roman ideas of worship. Holy Communion has echoes of a blood sacrifice. It is not necessary to receive Holy Communion to feel close to God. As a symbol it is not harmful, but it also not required. You come closer to God by being a good person rather than performing rituals. The idea of reincarnation was also taken out of the New Testament. This is a grave error. Reincarnation is fundamental to how the spiritual world works. There is no Hell full of burning fire.

At death everyone goes to the spirit world. Each soul has a review of their life with their spirit council who are there to guide them. The soul sees how well it performed its task for that lifetime. There is no judgement but just a sense of helping the soul to advance. In time the soul chooses a new body to undergo new experiences which will advance the soul. The aim is to become close to God. Archangels have achieved closeness to the Creator. They are messengers and carry out the will of God. Perfection of the spirit is achieved through many lifetimes.

There were teachers before Jesus who had come to wisdom through meditation. They are found in all cultures and times.

Jesus often spoke in parables and allegories. This was due to the constraints of the time in which he lived. The time has come for the truth to be known to everyone. The spirits can help us to see this truth.

The law is about love and kindness. It must be revealed little by little because it could dazzle people in the way a bright light can blind you. Old sacred writings of all religions have some truth in them, and they are worthy of study. These truths are mixed in with misunderstandings and falsehoods.

Moral law is about doing the right thing. You must distinguish between good and evil. It is the right thing when an action is done for the good of all. Intelligence of people allows them to know the difference between good and evil. The most important law is the one that Jesus said, "All things that you want men to do to you, you also must do to them." You will not go wrong if you make this your rule of action. This idea is often referred to as the Golden Rule.

The natural law guides you to your needs. If you eat too much you suffer for it. You must know when there is enough. It is the same in all things.

Evil exists because each person has free will. He must choose between good or evil. The spirit acquires experience through the body. Through experience he learns both good and evil. Some do evil because they do not know any better. It is worse when an enlightened person continues to do evil as he knows he should not do it.

People should strive not only to avoid evil but to do good things. This action is how to please God. You should be useful to others as much as you are able. If you find yourself surrounded with crime, you must resist it. It's a test. You must rise above your surroundings and provide a good influence on those around you.

Each action has a different level of virtue. The more difficult the action is the more merit the person receives. A poor man may give a morsel of bread to his friend. This action has a higher value than a rich man who donates money to the poor. Jesus told us about virtuous action in the parable of the widow's mite. In this story Jesus tells how rich people donate large sums to the temple. A poor widow comes along and puts two small coins into the box. Jesus tells his disciples that the widow gave more than all the others because she gave all she had.

Charity is the most important virtue and allows people to advance the most in their spiritual life.

One part of the law is that of adoration. This law means you should turn your thoughts towards God. This sentiment is innate in all peoples. True adoration is in your heart. God's eyes are always on you watching all your actions. You can adore God anywhere. Keep God in your thoughts all through the day.

It can be useful to engage in external acts of worship such as going to Church. Some do these actions purely for the sake of appearances and their actions do not match. Their hypocrisy causes great harm. God prefers to be worshipped from the heart. You can go to a religious building to worship, but you do not need to. You can worship in private. Worshipping with others who have similar thoughts and feelings has power to attract good spirits. This is why some religious buildings have such a good atmosphere. Others just seem like ordinary buildings.

A life of contemplation is not the best use of a life. Such a person may do nothing evil, but he also does nothing good. He must carry out his duties on Earth. Many religions have taught that to meditate on God is the most important thing to do in life. Some meditation is extremely useful, but the most important thing is to help other people. You cannot do this if you are sitting on a mountain top all day.

Prayer is useful if it comes from the heart. It is the intention that is the most important thing. It is better to pray from the heart than read one from a book. Prayer should be offered with faith, passion and sincerity. It should be conducted with repentance and humility. Prayer can praise, ask and thank. Prayer helps men to be stronger and to resist evil. Good spirits can assist a person praying with sincerity.

God can forgive bad conduct if the person chooses to change their behaviour. Good actions are the best prayers. You can pray for other people and the action of praying can attract good spirits to that person. You can pray for yourself but there are some things that must be gone through even though they are hard. God takes account of how well you have borne your trials. Prayer can help you to heed the good suggestions of your mind that can help you out of difficulties.

You can pray for the dead and the dead spirit will be consoled by your prayer, but you cannot alter the will of God by doing this. If the spirit must suffer in the next life because of what they have done in this one there is nothing, you can do to change that.

You can also pray to good spirits as they are the messengers of God. Their power still depends on God so prayers to them must be accepted by God if they are to be effective. People often pray to angels and saints, and this is fine to do but God alone has the power to change things or not.

The Lord's prayer that Yeshua taught us was originally spoken in Aramaic. Aramaic was Yeshua's native tongue. The translation in the

Bible does not give us the full sense of his meaning. Here is a more suitable rendering of it:

O Birther. Father and Mother of the Universe.

You create all that moves in light.

Focus your light within us. Make it useful as the rays of a beacon show the way.

Create your reign of unity now though our passionate hearts and willing hands.

Your desire then acts in harmony with ours as in all light and all forms.

Grant what we need each day in bread and insight.

We need subsistence for the call of growing life.

Loose the cords of mistakes binding us.

We release the strands we hold of others' guilt.

Done let us enter forgetfulness.

Free us from unripeness.

From you is born all ruling will, the power and the life to do.

The song that beautifies everything, from age to age renews.

Power to these statements.

May they be the source from which all actions grow.

Sealed in trust and faith.

There is only one God. In the past many people believed in polytheism. The gods they were worshipping were really spirits and not God.

Ancient people often practised human sacrifice. This idea is a primitive belief, and it is false. They had the idea that they must offer their most precious things to God and so gave human beings in sacrifice. God does not ask for sacrifices nor has he ever. He does not require animal or human sacrifice. When you read in the Bible or other religious texts about God asking for a human sacrifice you know this is not God but a mischievous spirit. Human and animal sacrifice is still going on today.

It is totally wrong, and nobody should take part in it. God does not ask for blood.

Religious wars are not the right thing to do. Other people should not be converted by force. These wars are stirred up by evil spirits. People engaging in such wars are in contradiction to the will of God which is to love your neighbour as yourself. The teachings of Jesus are best promoted through persuasion and gentleness, not with the sword. We know that violence happened during the Crusades when Christians wanted to convert Muslims but conversion by force is always a bad idea. Use gentle words and the example of your good life to persuade people to follow the right path.

God blesses those who do good. Helping the poor and afflicted is the best way to honour God. God loves simplicity. He does not need to be worshipped with pomp and ceremony. Many churches are extremely grand, and the cathedrals can be full of wealth. This opulence is also found in other religions. There is no need for this kind of building. You can worship in simplicity.

Labour is another law of nature. Civilisation requires those within it to labour so that they can meet their needs and enjoy life. The spirit also labours as much as the body. Any sort of useful occupation is labour. Labour allows a man to develop his intelligence. It is also an expiation. A person who is required to work hard in his life may be making amends for wrongdoing in his previous life. Each person must work according to their abilities. It is so important for people to receive the right kind of education so that they can find out where their true talents lie.

Rest is also necessary after labour. Each person must decide when he has done enough. It is a crime to impose too much labour on your underlings. This action goes against the law of God. A man is only obliged to labour according to his strength. The strong should work for the weak. If family cannot help, then society should step in to provide charity for those who cannot work.

There is also a law of reproduction. Reproduction is a law of nature. The Earth will never become too numerous as God will not allow it. Races grow and disappear, and other races take their place. The current race which is in the ascendant will die out. It will be replaced by other more perfect races. Anything that hinders reproduction artificially is not a good thing. Sex for the sake of sensuality takes place when the body is taking precedence over the soul. Matter is not more important than the spiritual life. In the current society sex is taking far too great a role and is causing harm in the world. Pornography is harmful and should be avoided. Concentrate on your spiritual life rather than giving too much time to sensuality.

Marriage is a good thing and a sign of progress. Marriage establishes solidarity between two people. To abolish marriage would be to return to a more primitive state. Those who are in conflict during marriage would be better to part. It is not necessary to remain married to the same person all your life if it is causing you suffering. Celibacy is not particularly pleasing to God if it arises from selfish motives. If a person is celibate to devote himself more fully to the service of humanity, then it is a good thing. Polygamy is not pleasing to God when it is based on sensuality. Marriage between two people is a step forward from polygamy.

There is a law of self-preservation. All living creatures have this instinct. God has made the Earth in a way that it allows all its inhabitants to have the necessities of life. When people do not have enough it is because they are not treating the Earth in the right way. People can find enough in a desert environment if they go about it in the right way. Many people waste the gifts of the Earth in frivolities and do not prepare for a time of famine.

If you cannot find enough for your needs, you must seek what you need. Mankind will be truly civilised when everyone has enough for their needs in the society. Each person must find the right path for them. If through no fault of your own, you find yourself without necessities you must bear your hardship with courage.

Nobody should give in to excess. Excess in anything brings suffering. Neither should people voluntarily deprive themselves. Doing good to others is more important than a vain pretence of doing without. There has been a tradition of extreme asceticism in the religious life but if such a life prevents a person from doing good to others, then it has no merit. Some fasting for short periods can be beneficial as it can bring you closer to God if you spend time in prayer and meditation.

Some religions prohibit the eating of certain foods, but this is not the law of God. A man can eat anything that is not injurious to his health. Animal foods are not forbidden and can give a man the strength he needs to do his labour. Listen to your body and find what foods suit you best. Some people might feel more suited to a vegetarian diet while others do not do so well on it. Each person must find the diet best suited to him rather than following arbitrary rules.

Self-flagellation is not required by God. We see harming the body in some religions of the world. In Christianity, people have scourged themselves in the hope that hurting the flesh will help the spiritual life. The Sadhus of India also indulge in mortifying the body. It is not necessary. It is better to do good to others. Work on your spiritual life by getting rid of your pride and selfishness.

There is a law of destruction. All things need to be destroyed so that they can be reborn and regenerated. Destruction is only a transformation. Living beings destroy each other for food which maintains the harmony of reproduction. The soul can never be destroyed, and it goes though many transformations. Men fear death so that they can preserve themselves. Through preserving themselves they can have beneficial experiences which will aid them on their spiritual journey. Men may kill animals but only for their right to food and safety. Wanton destruction of animals is not pleasing to God. Hunting for pleasure rather than for food is giving in to a low nature. It should be avoided. When a person undergoes a disaster, he is gaining spiritual advancement. Death is unimportant in the great scheme of things. A century on Earth is just a moment in eternity. The spiritual world is the real world. Spirits are the children of God and bodies are just envelopes.

Wars are caused by man giving in to his animal nature. It is barbaric to know no other right than that of the strongest. War lessens as people become more civilised. Wars will cease when men understand justice and practise the law of God. War has been useful sometimes in providing freedom and progress. If a man stirs up war for his own profit, he is in the wrong. He will have to undergo many painful existences to atone for his crime.

Murder is a great crime in the sight of God. Murdering another means you have interfered with that person's mission. Murder can be excused if it was self-defence. Infanticide is not acceptable to God. You should never kill children or babies nor perform abortions. Cruelty to people or animals is always wrong and a sign of an evil nature. Every person has a sense of right and wrong within him but in some people it is latent. It must be opened like a flower.

Humans are progressing towards good. Evil doers will gradually disappear. Each person through each incarnation will gain a clearer understanding of good and evil. Then the Earth will become a more harmonious place. Human beings will live in harmony with one another. They will seek to help other people, and everyone will have enough for their needs. In a well-ordered society, each person has food and shelter and any excess he has can be given to others. Each person finds his place and labours at something he enjoys.

Capital punishment is also wrong, and it will disappear in time. A criminal must be given the opportunity to repent. It is for God to exact justice. Those who have committed crimes will have to pay for them in their next incarnations until the crime is expiated.

There is a social law. It is necessary for people to have a social life. God made people to live in society which is why he gave them the power of speech. People instinctively seek society and progress is obtained in helping each other. It is not beneficial to live in total isolation. For spiritual progress to take place you must be useful to others and this kind of progress cannot take place when you are alone. It is selfish to live alone as the law of love and charity is forgotten. Each person must strive to find a community that is suited to him. If the community is lacking, then he must build it through good actions.

Silence can be useful. In silence you can gain possession of yourself, and your spirit is freer. All of this allows greater communication with the spirit world. However, there is no need to take a vow of silence. You have been given the power of speech for a reason. Communication allows you to do good to others.

Family ties are important in the law of God. Love of family helps people to love one another like they love their brothers. To ignore family ties is a form of selfishness. However, some people are born in to abusive and evil families. If this is the case, there is no need to stay within the family. You can make a new social group of more sympathetic people.

There is a law of progress. The state of nature is the state mankind finds himself in the beginning. He must progress beyond this through civilisation. People must progress and cannot return to the state of nature. Moral progress follows intellectual progress. Through using his intelligence man can recognise good and evil. Sometimes progress proceeds slowly but at other times there is turmoil and revolution which hastens progress. Out of evil good things can come. Pride and selfishness hinder progress. Men develop their intellects but can become ambitious and in love with riches. Eventually, they realise that there is a greater happiness beyond material enjoyments. Through reincarnation, people can gain more and more spiritual progress. They may have been in a primitive and poor state in their early incarnations, but they have developed themselves through each lifetime.

Eventually, civilisation will be purified. People will develop their moral nature as much as their intelligence. We have not achieved this state yet.

There is a need for a new religion. This is the religion we have been describing which encompasses the spirits. One day this will happen. The new faith will destroy materialism. People will understand that they can ensure their future happiness by the actions they take in their present life. Prejudices of sects, social position and colours will be destroyed, and everyone will be united like brothers.

There is a law of equality. All people are equal in the sight of God. Some spirits have lived more lives than others, so they have learned more and developed themselves more. Sometimes beings of the higher worlds come and dwell on Earth to teach by their example. Inequality in social conditions is due to the work of man, not God. Social inequality will disappear when pride and selfishness disappear. Those who use their own superior social position to oppress the weak will find that in their next incarnation it is their turn to be oppressed. It is not praiseworthy to seek after wealth and this is not pleasing to God. It is not possible for everyone to be equally rich as people have different aptitudes. It is better to spend your time doing something that you enjoy. In this way, everyone has a sense of wellbeing.

Poverty and wealth both provide opportunities for soul growth in different ways. Rich people could do good with their wealth, but they can tend to become selfish, proud and feel they never have enough. The poor must resign themselves to their fate while the rich must make good use of their wealth and power. Riches tend to attach people more closely to matter and keep them from spiritual perfection. This spiritual idea is why Yeshua said it is easier for a camel to go through the eye of a needle than for a rich man to enter Heaven.

Men and women are equal in the sight of God. Women are oppressed in some societies because of the actions of men. Men are often stronger, so they are more suited for rough work, but many women excel at gentler types of work. In some cases, a woman is strong enough to do manual labour like a man. There are some men who are more suited to traditionally female occupations. Each person, whether they be a man or a woman, should find their proper role in life that is suited to their personality and strength. They can both help each other through life.

There is equality in death. Those who have excessive funeral arrangements are full of pride. Often these kinds of arrangements are gratifying the need of relatives to parade their wealth. There is no need for grand funeral arrangements, and they will not aid the spiritual progress of the deceased person.

There is a law of liberty. Nobody is completely free because each person has need of others. Slavery is against the law of God. You should not own other people or mistreat them. Each person has the right to earn his living. Slavery will disappear as mankind progresses.

Everybody has freedom of thought. Conscience is an inner thought. People are responsible for their thoughts to God. Thoughts are good when they lead to the practice of goodness. People with erroneous beliefs should be persuaded with gentleness, never violence. Every person has free will. Without free will people are just machines. People in a primitive state are acting more from instinct than from free will. As a person develops his free will becomes stronger than instinct.

When bad things happen to people it can be because of their own actions. Sometimes, a soul has agreed to undergo trials before birth in the spirit state. If a life is a trial, you may see a good person having bad things occurring in their life through no fault of their own. They must bear their trials as best they can.

The hour of your death is appointed, and nothing can change it. You have been given the sense of caution about your safety to protect you and stop you from ending your life prematurely. Sometimes a brush with death can encourage the person to mend their ways and live in a better way.

No one is predestined to commit a crime. Someone who murders another does so from his own free will. He may have chosen before his incarnation to endure a life of hardship where murder was a possibility, but his trial is to resist evil actions even in the most trying of circumstances.

The future is hidden from people. In rare cases, God may allow the future to be revealed. If people knew the future, they would neglect to act in the present. It is best to concentrate on doing good in the present moment.

We are all responsible for our actions. Mischievous spirits may try to tempt us to do the wrong thing, but we must resist the temptation. We need to listen to the good spirits who are urging us to do good.

There is a law of justice. The sentiment of justice is perfectly natural. Justice is the respect for the rights of others. This law is just like what Jesus taught: do to others what you would do to yourself. If you follow the example of Jesus, you will be truly righteous.

The right to live is the most important right. Nobody has the right to take the life of another. Man does have the right to defend his property and wealth. It is selfishness if he amasses wealth purely for himself, but it is acceptable if he does it for his family or for the good of others.

Charity is important. This word means being kind to everyone, indulge the imperfections of others, forgive wrongdoing. Love and charity go along with the law of justice. Enemies must be forgiven. Give good when you receive evil and refrain from vengeance.

Begging can be degrading to a person. In a well organised society, each man should be given the means to live if he cannot work. True charity is gentle and kind. It should not be done in the spirit of pride or vanity. Relieve suffering without ostentation.

Maternal affection is a natural sentiment. We see it in animals but in humans it is even greater. It survives or the whole of life and even beyond death. Absence of motherly affection is sometimes a trial chosen by the child.

CHAPTER EIGHTEEN
MORAL PERFECTION

The highest of virtues is to sacrifice self-interest for the good of others. We might call this disinterested kindness. Some people are naturally kind because they have developed themselves spiritually in previous lifetimes. One day the Earth will be like this as everyone will have good intentions towards each other.

Imperfection is characterised by selfishness. Many people pretend to be virtuous, but they have selfish intentions underneath. Disinterested kindness is extremely rare on Earth. If you are attached to material things, you do not understand your true destiny.

People should do good spontaneously without thinking of the result. The act of goodness is to please God and to relive the suffering of other people. Every good act brings you nearer to God.

Rich people should use their wealth to help others rather than using it purely for selfish reasons. In Western society wealth is being held in too high a regard. Amassing money seems to be the only aim of many people. Money alone will not make you happy and attachment to material things stops your soul from ascending to a higher level. Learn to let go of the love of the material world and concentrate on your spiritual life. This idea is in the New Testament when Yeshua tells a rich man to give up all he owns to follow him. Have faith that God will provide for your basic needs and concentrate on helping others.

It is not good to criticise others. You should be aware of your own faults and try to rectify them. By practising virtue, you become a better person and you act as an example to other people. Raise people through your words and actions rather than criticism.

We all have passions which are a natural phenomenon. They can become evil in excess. Passion can aid you in accomplishing God's will but in excess they can crush you.

You can overcome excess passion yourself through effort and you can ask the spirits for help.

The worst vice is selfishness and all other vices flow from this. You must try to root out every selfish feeling. As you become more spiritual you become less enthralled with the world of matter. As this process happens you become less selfish.

When selfishness is rooted out people will live in harmony with each other like brothers. Education is key in bringing about a more moral and just world. Education should help people to find their true vocation. It should also teach them about morality and the truth of the spiritual world. Much of education today is severely lacking in this area and is even teaching children to do the wrong things. Education should be conducted in harmony with spiritual principles.

A truly virtuous man practises justice, love and charity. Such a person does good for its own sake. He is kind. He indulges the weakness of others as he knows he also has vices: let he who is without sin cast the first stone as Jesus said. He is not vindictive but forgives others.

To improve yourself it is important to understand yourself: know thyself. At the end of each day, you should examine your conscience.

Review the events of the day and evaluate your behaviour during each occurrence.

CHAPTER NINETEEN
JOYS AND SORROWS

Perfect happiness is never possible when you live on Earth. Bodily life is either a trial or an expiation. Man will be much happier when he obeys the laws of God. Much of our unhappiness stems from our own excesses. As we look back on our life, we can see the moment when we strayed from the right road and more and more trouble ensued from that moment.

To be happy you need the necessities of human life. You also need a good conscience and a belief in a future state. Misfortunes must be born with resignation. Those evil people who seem to be enjoying good fortune will have a reversal of luck on a later date, perhaps in the next life.

It is also necessary to follow your true vocation to be happy. Sadly, parents will often force a child on a path that is not right for him. Pride often prevents people from finding a more suitable occupation. In a society in accordance with the principles that Jesus set out nobody would die of hunger.

Much unhappiness is caused by being too attached to the things of this world. Raise your thoughts towards the infinite. The petty troubles of human existence then seem insignificant. Everyone can be consoled that they have a better future.

It is not wrong to talk to spirits of the dead if you are serious and sincere in the communication. The spirits delight in talking to you. We should be glad on the death of a loved one that they have been released from their prison and patiently wait until we too are free.

You are never alone as the spirits are always around you and you can communicate with them any time. Just sit quietly and talk to them. You can speak to them just like a normal conversation. You don't need special words. Tell them what you want them to know and ask them for help.

Do not be concerned about ungrateful or unkind people. Keep doing good to people anyway. Jesus himself was treated badly by other people and so will you be. People who behave badly will be punished later.

There are two kinds of attraction between people: that of the body and of the soul. The affection of the soul is long lasting but that of the body will fade away. Spend time with people who make your soul feel good. Seek out those who have things in common with you. Lust is only of the body. A good relationship must involve the spirit.

There is no need to be afraid of death. Death has no terrors. Become spiritually minded and the spirit becomes calm and serene.

Suicide is not acceptable. To avoid this feeling, it is necessary to find some useful aim in harmony with your natural aptitudes. Bear the sorrows of life with patience and resignation. Know that there is a better life to come.

If a person has driven someone to suicide, they will be punished heavily. Each person must bear adversity bravely and not worry about social position. It is better to work as a labourer than commit suicide after having lost social position.

Most peoples who have lived on the Earth have believed in some kind of life after death. It is a natural thing for men to think. Perfected spirits experience pure happiness after death. They know all things. They don't feel hatred or jealousy or envy or ambition. They have mutual affection for each other. They have no material wants. They aid the progress of other spirits.

There is no hell as has been described by the church. Those who do evil feel guilt and remorse after death when they look back on their life. They will suffer in subsequent incarnations for what they have done.

A good future after death is achieved by doing good actions regardless of your religion or beliefs while on Earth. Nobody is punished for not knowing the truth about the spirit world as many have no way of knowing.

A spirit is not released from suffering after death. If he has done bad things he will suffer morally as a spirit. When he is reincarnated, he may have hard trials to undergo. If he has been harsh to his underlings, he will find himself with a harsh master in a future life.

As a spirit is purified, it is reincarnated into purer worlds. Eventually the spirits become fully purified spirits in the presence of God.

It is important to repent within the bodily life if you realise you have done wrong. Then you can make reparations for your sins. Repentance does not mean you are absolved. You will still have to face trials for what you have done in future incarnations.

All spirits will eventually progress, repent and give up their evil actions. Some take longer to do this than others.

There is no eternal punishment. There is no Hell that is taught by some religions. The words of Yeshua on this subject were changed by others who had their own evil purposes. In times past it was easier to control people when you could frighten them with eternal torment. These days most people reject the idea and then end up leaving the spiritual life completely. After death you review your life for good or ill and you choose the next life to advance your spirit. It may involve suffering and misfortune to atone for wrong actions, but it will not last forever and your soul can progress to better things. God is just and good. He would never do that.

The aim of human existence is union with God. To attain this there must be knowledge, love and justice. Ignorance, hatred and injustice work against this aim.

Much of church dogma has obscured the truth. The doctrine of the resurrection of the body is really a reference to reincarnation. The spirits now want to speak plainly about the truth of the spiritual world and not in allegories. The body is not resurrected but the spirit is in a new body. The resurrection does not take place on the last day but is taking place all the time.

Heaven and hell are only symbols. There are both happy and unhappy spirits in the spiritual world.

We are approaching a time when the earth will be transformed. This will happen when there are more good people than bad upon the Earth.

CHAPTER TWENTY
THE GOSPEL ACCORDING TO MALALIA

There was great tribulation in the land of Israel. The Romans had invaded the land. They came from the sea and became masters of the Jews. They defiled the places of worship and installed their own false gods. The women were used by the Roman soldiers and the Jews were living like slaves. The Israelites were full of weeping. They turned to God and asked for help.

God, the eternal and supreme being, heard the cry of the Jews in pain. A part of the supreme being, the great spirit, broke off from his state of bliss and incarnated in human form to help the Israelites. His aim was to teach mankind to identify with God and obtain eternal happiness. He wanted to show by example how to improve your moral purity so you can ascend to perfection and enter Heaven in eternal bliss.

The great spirit was born in Israel. His mother Mary had been taken by a Roman soldier, who was from Greece, and he used her as his concubine. Mary became pregnant. On hearing the news, the soldier threw her into the street. Mary returned to her family home. Joseph, an upright man, was a friend to this poor family. He took Mary as his wife even though she was with child as he received a dream from the angel Gabriel telling him to marry Mary and the child would be holy. The child will be called Yeshua, also called Jesus and Issa.

Yeshua was born in Bethlehem. Joseph and Mary had travelled there to be counted for Roman taxes but when they arrived, they could find no lodging. They took shelter in a stable and Mary gave birth to Yeshua there. Three wise men travelled from northern India, the border with Tibet, the land of snows, as they had received a sign that a great king was to be born in the land of Israel. They went to King Herod Antipas and asked: "Where is the king of the Jews?" Herod consulted his priests who told him a great leader was prophesied to be born in Bethlehem. He sent the wise men to Bethlehem, and they found Yeshua in the stable under a great white star. They gave him gifts of gold, frankincense and myrrh and kneeled to worship him. They were warned by the angels in a dream not to go back to Herod and they returned home by a different way.

Yeshua was in great danger from Herod, who wanted to kill him, so Joseph took his family to Egypt where they stayed until the death of the king. Joseph received a dream that Herod was no more, and he returned to Israel and settled in Nazareth. The family were poor people and Joseph worked as a carpenter. They were virtuous people, and they instructed their son in the ways of the Jewish religion. They also had other children.

Yeshua grew and was filled with the eternal spirit. He talked of the one God from the earliest age and urged people to repent and purify their souls. People came from all over the land to hear him and marvel at his words. Jesus came of age at thirteen. He knew that his path would not be the usual one. He left Nazareth and journeyed with a train of merchants to India. He wanted to perfect himself for his mission and study the ways of the great teachers of the East.

He arrived in India and settled among the devotees of the god Jain. Yeshua saw that these people were in error with their god, so he left them and went to Odisha to live with the priests of Brahma. They were

Hindus. Here Yeshua read the Vedas and was instructed in to how to understand them. He learned to cure ailments and to drive out evil desires from men. Everyone loved Yeshua because he loved the poor and taught them the wisdom of the Vedas. This teaching angered the Brahmins who said the low castes were not to hear the holy scriptures. Yeshua argued with them and said all people are equal in the sight of God. He taught the poor of the lowest caste that there is only one God who created all things. God created Man and breathed divinity into him. He also taught them that it is wrong to worship idols. God does not reside in images of stone nor metal. Yeshua taught that one day the Brahmins will be reduced to the lowest of the low and the low will be raised up. He also told them that the Vedas did not contain the whole truth as they had been altered. Yeshua told the people to be humble and to help each other. They should not be envious of those who have more.

The Brahmins planned to kill Jesus for his words, but he was warned of this by his students and went into the mountains of Nepal. Here Yeshua lived among the Buddhists. In this place Yeshua learned Pali and studied the sacred Sutras. He stayed for six years learning in the monastery at Hemis which was then Tibet. Yeshua left the Himalayas and journeyed westwards. He preached to everyone about how people could gain perfection through purifying themselves through good words and actions. Pure souls will die with their wrongdoing forgiven and they can dwell with God. He also taught that it was wrong to worship images. The great spirit cannot be contained in stone or metal.

Yeshua taught against the ritual sacrifice of animals or people. He condemned the priests who had led his children astray from the true path. Everything is filled with God and should not be sacrificed.

Yeshua taught the pagans how to purify themselves. They must open their hearts to God. They must not tell lies or give in to excess of anything including food and sex. In this way they can achieve supreme bliss.

Yeshua travelled on and came into Persia. He taught people who were Zoroastrians. They believed that Saint Zoroaster was the only true god. The priests spoke against Yeshua but the people loved him and listened to his words. Yeshua told the people not to worship the sun. God created the sun as he did everything else. Yeshua warned that the priests would be punished for spreading false ideas. When the priests heard Yeshua speak against them, they threw him out of the city walls. Yeshua was protected by God from the dangers of wild animals and went on his way.

Yeshua returned to Israel when he was twenty-nine years old. He found the people of Israel in an even worse state than when he left them. He began to teach the people all over the land.

At the same time there was a preacher in Judea called John the Baptist. He was telling people to repent of their sins and baptising them in the River Jordan. He wore a rough coat of camel hair tied with a leather belt and he lived on locusts and wild honey. Yeshua came to see John and he was baptised in the river. John was a holy man who know who Yeshua was. He didn't think he was worthy to baptise Yeshua, but he was persuaded. At that moment a great light descended on Yeshua and a voice said, "This is my beloved son in whom I am well pleased."

Yeshua continued to teach the people. He warned against the worship of idols. He told them to help the poor, feed them and heal their sick. Yeshua told them that the real temples were not buildings but human hearts. Hearts are purified by thinking good thoughts and having faith in God. Loving thoughts and kindness are the ways to God. Do good actions with no thought of reward.

Yeshua taught all over the land and thousands of people came to hear him. He then came up to Jerusalem to preach in the temple. He warned the people that darkness had descended on them because they had lost their faith. The light will return as people unite. He told them to look after each other. Their patience would be rewarded with supreme bliss. They were exhorted to pray to the one true God and not to consult oracles or mediums.

Yeshua also taught them to respect their wives and mothers. He said that women could soften the hearts of men and draw the evil out of them. Bless and adore women as they are your only friends on Earth. Love your wives and submit to them. Women are precious treasures. Never humiliate a woman and protect her from harm.

Yeshua performed miracles at this time. He healed the sick, raised the near dead, cured the blind and fed people with manifestation of bread. He could walk on water and calm storms. He had a band of twelve special followers, but he also preached to thousands out in the open. The people loved him, and his fame spread far and wide.

The governor of Judea, Pontius Pilate, became uneasy about Yeshua as he feared a revolution. He thought Yeshua was a political leader rather than a spiritual one. He thought Yeshua would become king in the land instead of him. He sent his soldiers to arrest Yeshua, and the great man was thrown into jail. While in jail he was tortured in the most horrible of ways and became physically weak.

Pilate organised a council of the elders to judge Yeshua. Pilate asked Yeshua if he was the king of the Jews and if he had come to incite a revolution against the Romans. Yeshua answered that he had not preached revolution but told people about the King of Heaven. He had told people to obey the laws of the land but to find peace within their hearts.

Pilate had bribed a man to come and speak against Yeshua. The man said Yeshua had told the people he was King of the Jews and that God had sent him to prepare the people. Yeshua knew that the man had been bribed and he told Pilate that he should not tell inferiors to lie to condemn an innocent man. Pilate flew into a rage and ordered the death of Yeshua. The Council of Jewish Elders argued that they could not condemn an innocent man, but Pilate would not listen to them. The Elders washed their hands in a ritual and left.

Yeshua was taken to be crucified on a cross with two robbers. Yeshua lost consciousness and was presumed dead. He was taken down from the cross at dusk and placed in a tomb. The next day the tomb was found to be empty.

The followers of Jesus spread all over the world and taught all the people the words of Jesus. They were to love God and each other to purify their souls. In this way they could achieve eternal bliss.

Yeshua did not die on the cross but came back to life from a coma. He was taken from the tomb and nursed back to health by his female followers and angels who came to his aid. Yeshua used the yogic techniques he had learned in the East to survive the crucifixion. The Tibetans call this the Rainbow Body. He was revived and appeared to his followers in several locations. It was too dangerous for him to remain in Israel, so he set out for India with his mother and Mary Magdalene. Mother Mary died along the way. Yeshua and Mary Magdalene settled in Kashmir where they lived quietly until old age. They had children together. Yeshua found work as a spiritual advisor to a great king. He also healed the sick and taught the people around him.

Such was the life of Yeshua, best of the sons of men. He is with you always even to the end of the world.

CHAPTER TWENTY-ONE

CONCLUSION

This book has shown you the truth of the spiritual world. It is hard to know what to call this true religion. Perhaps spiritualism or the truth of the spirits might be appropriate terms. Yeshua called his teachings The Way. The reality of the spirit world goes beyond the usual fare of psychics and fortune tellers who often only understand a little of what they are doing. Spiritualism is often mocked as frivolous and the work of charlatans but true communication with spirits gives great knowledge and allows humanity to move forward.

Spiritualism is against materialism. It demonstrates the existence and the immortality of the soul. This gives hope for the future. The progress of humans relies on justice, love and charity. The doctrine of the spirits is identical to the true words of Jesus Christ. The spirits speak the truth without the need for allegory or symbols. His words are no longer twisted by those who wished to use his name for personal power and glory.

The good spirits urge us to be kind to all. They are friends with those who do good. Jesus is also friends with those who do good. The road we are following will lead us to God.

Through love we raise ourselves.

With all love,

Malalia

www.ingramcontent.com/pod-product-compliance
Lightning Source LLC
Chambersburg PA
CBHW052206070526
44585CB00017B/2087